AF530062

# Understanding the Subtle Realities of Life

**Sreejit Sreedharan**

Qurate
qurateBooks.com

**Understanding the Subtle Realities of Life**
Sreejit Sreedharan



Published in 2025

© Published by

Qurate
qaratebooks.com

**Qurate Books Pvt. Ltd.**
Goa 403523, India
www.qaratebooks.com
Tel: 1800-210-6527, Email: info@qaratebooks.com



**ISBN: 978-93-5898-131-5**

# Contents

# Introduction

I have never believed in cosmic forces or God since childhood. I was born into a middle-class family in the state of Kerala, which is also called 'God's Own Country'. My parents taught me all the mythological stories since I was hardly five years old. They taught me the Ramayan and the Mahabharata, as well as the various tales related to the Devis and the Devatas.

But I never believed in any of them. I often wondered how the heavenly bodies like the Sun, the Moon and other planets can have a human form. My mother told me that the Sun has a human form and he is riding on a chariot which the seven horses manoeuvre. And I used to look up at the sky and observe the Sun. Do I see any human riding on a chariot run by the seven horses? I just saw a big ball of fire, which is quite bright and resplendent.

I was not satisfied with the description of the Sun given in the Hindu mythology. I started questioning others whether they had seen any God in their personal life. I never got any satisfactory answer from any one of them. This turned me into an atheist.

Till I was 16 years old, I was an atheist. But something changed in my life after I completed my S.S.C. Board examinations. I got introduced to a famous personality in India who is known for being an atheist himself, and who got transformed when he met a saint who is known for his madness towards God. And that famous personality is none other than the cyclonic monk Swami Vivekananda.

I was inquisitive about his life story. I wanted to know how a die-hard atheist like Narendranath Dutta (Swami Vivekananda's original name) can be transformed into a believer in God just by meeting an uneducated saint named Shri Ramakrishna Paramahamsa. I read Swami Vivekananda's biography and learnt that through certain spiritual practices like meditation, we can realise God.

I started observing strict celibacy in thought, word and deed. Celibacy is considered to be the sine qua non for spiritual development. I stopped watching television where there are too many distractions, and focused entirely on the practice of meditation.

Initially, I was able to meditate for only 15 minutes. I used to sit in a yogic posture named 'Padmasana', keeping my hands in Dhyan mudra. After 15 minutes, my legs developed cramps, which often subside after relaxing my leg muscles. Slowly and steadily, I was able to meditate for half an hour.

It was not easy to meditate for half an hour. The mind is highly uncontrollable, and keeping the body in a still position for a long time requires regular practice and strong willpower. But I had unwavering faith in myself and in all my learnings that I have imbibed after reading several spiritual books. I want to realise God. I want to enter into the state of super consciousness or Samadhi.

Gradually, I was able to meditate for nearly one hour. One night, when I was meditating in a dark room, I got my first spiritual experience. A dazzling light appeared on my forehead, which permeated the whole body like an electric current. The Kundalini energy got activated. I was frightened by this spiritual experience, but it also turned me into a believer in the Almighty God.

When I used to be an atheist, I was quite arrogant. I abhor touching the feet of an elderly person because I was egotistical. When my Kundalini energy got aroused, my ego got smashed. For the first time, I touched the holy feet of Lord Ayyappa and surrendered myself. I started practising meditation with more faith and dedication.

Once while meditating, I lost my body consciousness. I felt as if I didn't have any physical body. After a few minutes, I regained my body consciousness. After a few days, I had my third spiritual experience. It happened when I was meditating on the Spiritual Master Mata Amritanandamayi. I visualised that she is seated in the same meditational pose as I am. Then I visualised that she is slowly entering my body. The moment I visualised that she had completely entered my body, that very moment my heart started beating very fast, which eventually turned into a normal heartbeat.

These spiritual experiences changed the whole perspective on life. Life has taught me so much at a very young age. I have read thousands of books, but my knowledge is not limited to mere book learning. I have practised the great principles that are written in those books and found them to be authentic. I have learnt the subtle aspects of life through thorough experimentation.

What you are going to read in this book in the upcoming pages is something which I have learnt through my own life experiences. I am not a saint. I did encounter spiritual experiences in my personal life, but those experiences were for my Self-Transformation and not for running away from worldly life. If I had never had those spiritual experiences, I would have still remained an atheist and spent my whole life criticising God and religion.

Whatever has happened so far in my life was for my good. I had more negative experiences in my life than positive ones. I had suffered from severe psychological problems in the past and had even been admitted to a lunatic asylum. I craved for money and success, but life only gave me fiascos. I had a few successes in my life, but they were short-lived and temporary.

Despite having so many negative experiences, I still value my life. I understood that whatever had happened in my life was making me strong and resilient. I no longer complain about life. I no longer get disappointed when I lose a job or lose my money. Because I view these so-called negative experiences as passing phases of life. I don't even get too much elevated when I get success in life because I consider these so-called positive experiences also as passing phases of life.

In this book, I am going to explain the subtle realities of life. If you understand these subtle realities, you will no longer complain about life. You will never get disappointed by your failures. You will start living effortlessly. You will start enjoying every moment of your life. You will start spending more time pursuing your passion rather than spending time on cheap thrills and entertainment. You will stop wasting your precious time on the trivialities of life.

I wish all my readers a life that is filled with great learning. I wish all my readers to reach the tremendous heights of Self-Actualisation, which is the ultimate goal of human life.

# 1

# Whatever Happens, Happens for Good

**LORD KRISHNA SAYS,** "Whatever happened, happened for the good. Whatever is happening is happening for good. Whatever will happen will also be for good." Is there any truth to this statement?

Whenever something unfavourable happens in our lives, we often lose faith in this statement. We often become pessimistic and miserable. It is because we give too much importance to the events. Success is an event. Likewise, failure is also an event. Whenever life gives you success, we tend to become too elevated. At the same time, when life gives you a series of fiascos, we tend to become depressed.

Our state of mind is determined by the events that are taking place in our lives. We are mere puppets in the hands of events that life offers us.

Why do bad events happen to good people? Why do we encounter failures, despite our hard work and perseverance? Why don't things go as per our plan?

The answer to these questions lies in the fact that life is full of dualities. Where there is joy, there is sorrow. Where there is success, there are failures. Where there is good, there is evil. I will talk about these dualities of life in detail in Chapter 2.

I want to tell you a story which explains that whatever happens in our lives is actually for our good.

*There was once a poor farmer who was known for his wisdom. He has seen the ups and downs of life and realised that whatever happens in life is for the highest good.*

*The farmer had a horse that helped him in his farming. One day, the horse ran away to the forest.*

*All the villagers took pity on him and consoled him, "We are sorry to hear this. This is such bad luck."*

*But the farmer responded, "Bad luck. Good luck. Who knows."*

*After a few days, the horse returned to the farmer. But it was not alone. He brought back 10 more horses along with him. Now the farmer had 11 horses in his custody.*

*All the villagers congratulated him, saying, "Oh! This is such good luck."*

*But the farmer replied, "Bad luck. Good luck. Who knows."*

*The 10 horses were wild, and now it is the responsibility of the farmer to tame them. The farmer had a son who helped him tame the horses.*

*One day, while taming one of the horses, the boy fell and injured his knees. The doctors advised him to complete bed rest for at least a month.*

*The villagers came to commiserate with the farmer and said, "This is such bad luck."*

*But the farmer remained stoical and responded, "Bad luck. Good luck. Who knows."*

*A few days later, war broke out in the village. The army was recruiting all the able-bodied young men to join them. The farmer's young son was not allowed to join the army because of his disability.*

*All the villagers came by and said, "You are so fortunate. This is such good luck."*

*But the farmer, as usual, responded, "Bad luck. Good luck. Who knows."*

This story explains that whatever appears as bad luck or misfortune might be for your highest good. Life never really goes as per our plan. It always works as per the Divine Plan.

As long as our intentions are good, nothing bad can happen in our lives. There will be temporary setbacks and failures, but we learn to move on and embrace the next chapter of life.

But if we hold on to the negative events of life and complain about them, then life will become miserable. I, too, held the negative events in my mind for a long time and had to be admitted to a mental hospital in Borivali. I am telling this from my personal experience.

When I was in school, I was bullied by a student for being too effeminate. I was an awkward person who lacked social skills. I always preferred to remain isolated. And that created a lot of frustration and inner turmoil. I was always an average student in my school and college days. In my first year of engineering, I got a drop for not clearing the examination. I lacked self-confidence and used to worry a lot.

When I was working with an IT company named Teradata, I couldn't clear their 4 certifications on the first attempt. Somehow, I cleared them before the six-month probation period. But I was mentally and physically exhausted and couldn't concentrate on the work. When the appraisals were announced, I was marked as 'Needs Improvement'. I was ultimately told to give my resignation. After that, I became mentally and emotionally disturbed. I started throwing tantrums in my house. I was filled with immense anger whenever I remembered all the negative experiences that I encountered in my life.

My parents took me to a mental hospital and admitted me there for one month. I was leading a miserable life. It took many years to come out of my depression. One of the factors which helped me to come out of depression is the practice of Vipassana meditation. Vipassana helped me to gain a better perspective on life. I will explain about Vipassana in Chapter 6.

Another factor which helped me to come out of depression was the Ayurvedic treatment which I went through in Kerala. I was given Abhyanga, or body massage, for a complete month. I also underwent the treatment of Shiro Dhara, which helped me to stabilise my mind.

Today, I am completely fine and leading a normal life. All those negative experiences which I had in my life helped me to gain control over my mind. My mind is now filled with immense gratitude for all the blessings which God has given me.

Contentment is highly indispensable for inner peace of mind. A person who is not satisfied with his life will always remain restless, no matter how many luxuries he is surrounded with. On the other hand, a person who is satisfied with whatever God has given him, no matter how little, will always remain peaceful.

If life only offered us positive experiences, then we would become egotistical. The negative experiences allow us to remain grounded. When things don't go well, we tend to remember God more. The negative experiences also make us resilient. The failures help us to build the inner quality of fortitude. We tend to become unflappable.

I will tell another story, which will make you understand why negative experiences are also imperative for our inner growth and spiritual progress.

*Once, a young boy saw a butterfly emerging from the cocoon. The butterfly was trying hard to emerge from the small hole of the cocoon.*

*No matter how hard it tried, the butterfly was not able to come out of the cocoon.*

*The boy decided to help the butterfly. He took a pair of scissors and cut open the shell of the cocoon. The butterfly was now able to come out of the cocoon.*

*But unfortunately, the butterfly was not able to unfurl its wings and fly gracefully. The butterfly spent the rest of its life crawling around with deformed wings.*

*What the boy in his kindness and haste did not understand was that the restricting cocoon and the struggle required for the butterfly to get through the small opening of the cocoon are nature's way of forcing fluid from the body of the butterfly into its wings, so that it would be ready for flight once it achieved its freedom from the cocoon.*

So, when life throws negative experiences, know that they are also for our highest good. Negative experiences make us mentally strong, while positive experiences add flavour to our lives. Both experiences are necessary in our journey of life.

# 2

# Dualities of Life

**LIFE IS FULL** of vicissitudes. It throws a series of challenges at us, constantly creating disruption and inner turmoil. However, without these challenges, life becomes meaningless.

Life is never a linear path. It is full of all kinds of ups as well as downs. It is full of all kinds of dualities. If there is life, there is death. If there is day, there is night. If there is success, there are failures. If there is beauty, there is ugliness. If there is strength, there is weakness. If there is health, there is also sickness.

We cannot just experience the positive aspects of life. We have to undergo the negative aspects as well. Sometimes, we experience only the positive aspects, and we end up being complacent and entering our comfort zone. But that creates inertia or laziness. We stop learning. We stop every scope for self-improvement or self-actualisation. We will be surrounded by all kinds of physical comforts and luxuries, but there will be no zest for life.

Even animals get all kinds of creature comforts. But there is no scope for achieving the higher dimensions of life in an animal. For life to become meaningful, challenges are highly indispensable. Without challenges, without these negative experiences, we can never embark on the journey toward self-actualisation.

We generally tend to avoid these negative experiences because they offer innumerable discomfort and unpleasant sensations to our body and mind. But we forget that these unpleasant sensations are imperative for our inner growth and spiritual development.

Anybody can be happy when situations are good. But to be happy amid life's vicissitudes is a sign of a highly evolved soul. Life's negative experiences make us stronger. It makes us unflappable. It makes us resilient.

I am not saying that you should not have positive experiences and embrace only the negative. We all want happiness, inner peace, enjoyment, and sense pleasure. But we should never get attached to any of these positive experiences because they are ephemeral by nature.

But the problem is that we develop a craving for these evanescent sense pleasures and work for our whole life just to enjoy them. Craving is the main cause of all our miseries. As long as we have a craving for momentary happiness, we will never experience real peace. These cravings produce 'vasanas' or subtle impressions in our subconscious mind. It is these 'samskara vasanas' that are the cause of our incessant rebirths into this material world.

To exhaust these 'vasanas' is the real purpose of human life. But it is not so easy to exhaust our 'vasanas' because our mind is highly uncontrollable and restless.

Through silence and meditation, we slowly start gaining some control over our minds. The practice of silence and meditation awakens the Law of Pure Potentiality, wherein creative ideas are generated by themselves. I underwent the 10-day Vipassana meditation course on 30th May 2012 at Dhamma Giri, situated at Igatpuri in the state of Maharashtra.

In the first 3 days, we practised Anapanasati meditation. During Anapanasati meditation, we focus our attention on the incoming and outgoing breath. We never regulate our breath like we do in Pranayama. The practice of Anapanasati meditation helps one to gain some control over the turbulent mind.

On the fourth day, we learned the technique of Vipassana meditation. We were told to observe the sensations of our body, starting from the crown of our head to the tip of our toes. Then we reverse the order and observe the sensations from the tip of our toes to the crown of our head.

As we continue to observe these sensations, we realise that they are ephemeral by nature. They just come and pass by. Sometimes, there are pleasant sensations, and sometimes, there are unpleasant sensations. Vipassana meditation aims to develop equanimity towards the various sensations that arise in our body.

We don't develop any kind of craving for pleasant sensations. We don't develop any kind of aversion to unpleasant sensations. We maintain equanimity towards both positive as well as negative sensations that arise in our body.

In life, we have to undergo both positive as well as negative experiences. But these experiences are temporary, and we have to keep moving on in our lives and keep learning what life wants to teach us through these experiences.

According to the Bhagavad Gita, this material world is *duḥkhālayam aśāśvatam*. It means that this world is full of misery and is temporary. There is no real joy in this material world. You may be the richest person on this planet, but life's dualities will still bind you. You will be bound by bodily pangs like hunger, thirst, old age, and disease.

In Buddhism, these bodily pangs are known as 'tanha'. As long as there is 'tanha', there will be miseries. Look at the lives of celebrities surrounded by all kinds of luxury and material comfort. You will find only external joy and glamour. But deep within themselves, they are restless and have no inner peace. Because their 'tanha' is at the extreme level. They can satisfy all their cravings and mindlessly splurge their money on momentary sense pleasures.

The story of Yayati proves this point. Yayati was an emperor who was also a great scholar and had immense erudition of the scriptures. He had a gorgeous wife named Devyani and had an affair with a maid named Sharmishtha. He was the father of five sons from two women. Yet Yayati unabashedly declares, 'My lust for pleasure is unsatisfied.'

Real happiness comes from reducing our cravings and focusing more on our inner development, which comes from self-mastery. When we focus our minds on learning new skills and upgrading ourselves, we slowly start developing detachment towards momentary thrills and excitement.

I am not saying to leave this material world and go to the forest to practice meditation. You will still live in this world, but your mind will be focused on a higher goal. You will no longer be disturbed by the worldly gossip. You will no longer be agitated by the trivialities of life.

Self-mastery is not easy. It requires discipline and unwavering dedication. You are bound to make mistakes and encounter multiple fiascos, but you move on because your focus is on a higher purpose and not on your mistakes and failures.

Life is all about learning. Become a lifelong learner and keep improving at every stage of life. That is the secret of true happiness.

# 3

# Failures are Inevitable

**IN THIS CHAPTER,** I will discuss famous personalities who have failed in life. Today, the whole world considers them to be the most successful. But there was a time when they only encountered severe fiascos, which could shatter any normal individual.

After learning about their failures, we will realise why failures are inevitable in our journey towards leading a successful life.

Elon Musk is currently the richest man in the world with a net worth of $332 billion. He is a businessman known for his leadership of Tesla, SpaceX, and X. But Elon Musk's journey to success was filled with setbacks and failures. When Elon graduated from college, he applied for a job at Netscape. But he was rejected. He decided to start his own company, Zip2, which is a software business for online city guides.

However, he got fired from his own company. He took all the earnings from Zip2 and co-founded X.com, an online payment company. X.com got merged with Confinity, and the company was renamed PayPal in 2001. Elon Musk was fired from PayPal due to disagreements over strategy and the company's direction. Despite this, when eBay bought PayPal for $1.5 billion, Musk walked away with a fortune—but he wasn't ready to retire.

After selling PayPal, Elon Musk founded SpaceX in 2002 and also became a major early investor and CEO of Tesla. Additionally, he co-founded Neuralink in 2016, a neurotechnology company.

After years of work, SpaceX launched its first Falcon 1 rocket in 2006. It exploded less than a minute after take-off. SpaceX launched the second rocket in 2007, but it was also a disaster. Investors started getting nervous.

SpaceX launched the third rocket, which also turned out to be a fiasco. NASA satellites were onboard this time, making the failure even worse. SpaceX was running out of money and about to go bankrupt. Just as SpaceX was about to collapse, NASA awarded the company a $1.6 billion contract. This single deal saved SpaceX, and Musk finally had hope.

Elon Musk's Tesla company also had a massive problem. Model S batteries kept catching fire. In 2015, a Falcon 9 rocket exploded on launch—this time with NASA cargo on board. In 2016, there was another major rocket failure. A rocket carrying Facebook's $200M satellite blew up on the launchpad.

Through all of these struggles, Elon Musk never gave up. Instead, he kept pushing forward, learning from every mistake. The lesson? Failure isn't the end—it's just another step toward success.

Joanne Rowling, known by her pen name J. K. Rowling, is a famous British author and philanthropist. She wrote the popular and critically acclaimed Harry Potter Series, which turned her into a millionaire with a net worth of around $1 billion. She was named the first billionaire author by Forbes in 2004.

But her early life was filled with setbacks and failures. She was nearly homeless and had financial difficulties. Her first marriage was a disaster, which eventually led to divorce in the year 1995. She had suffered from bouts of depression because of her life's difficulties.

She had experienced numerous rejections from publishers after finishing her first novel. These rejections, while discouraging, did not deter her from pursuing her dream of becoming an author. Rowling's unwavering determination and belief in her story eventually led to the publication of the first Harry Potter novel in 1997.

Most people quit after encountering a few failures. And that is the main reason why most people are unsuccessful. Failure is an inevitable part of life and can be a valuable learning experience. Perseverance and resilience are crucial for overcoming adversity and achieving one's goals. Seeking support from friends and family can provide the strength needed to persevere during challenging times.

Amitabh Bachchan is known as the Indian Film Industry's Megastar. He has a net worth of $415 million. But his journey towards success was filled with difficulties and challenges. He was rejected by All India Radio for his baritone voice. He faced numerous rejections when he moved to Mumbai and struggled to find work. He even slept on the streets due to a lack of accommodation.

After entering the film business in 1969, he featured in as many as 12 flop films before getting his first hit in the 1973 blockbuster Zanjeer. At the time he was shooting Coolie in 1983, Big B was at the height of stardom. However, on the film set, he had a brush with death during the filming of a stunt scene.

In the late 1990s, Amitabh Bachchan Corporation Limited (ABCL), Bachchan's production company, went bankrupt, leading to a significant financial crisis. This resulted in 55 legal cases against him and a debt of Rs. 90 crore.

In 2000, a heavily debt-ridden Big B turned to Yash Chopra and requested him to be cast in Mohabbatein. With the success of the film, his debt declined. He reinvented himself and embraced new opportunities, ultimately solidifying his position as a leading actor. His resilience and ability to overcome adversity are key to his success story.

Failure is an inevitable part of life and a necessary component of growth. By reframing failure as a learning opportunity and adopting a growth mindset, individuals can learn from their mistakes, build resilience, and ultimately achieve greater success.

I would like to end this chapter with a famous quote of Swami Vivekananda:

*Never mind failures; they are quite natural; they are the beauty of life--these failures. What would life be without them? It would not be worth having if it were not for the struggles. Where would be the poetry of life? Never mind the struggles, the mistakes. I never heard a cow tell a lie, but it is only a cow---never a man. So never mind these failures, these little backslidings; hold the ideal a thousand times; and if you fail a thousand times, make the attempt once more.*

# 4

# Fallacy of Hard Work

**OUR PARENTS AND** teachers have told us from childhood to work hard. We were told that working hard is the only path towards success. But unfortunately, hard work is not the only criterion which leads to success. Other factors like talent, opportunity, luck, and strategic efforts also play significant roles.

I also believed that hard work is the only essential factor which leads to success. When I was in school and college, I had burned the midnight oil just for the sake of cramming my study material. But I never got substantial success in my exams. Because I used to give my exams in a state of lethargy.

When I was working in a reputed IT company named Teradata, I couldn't clear my certification exams on the first attempt. Eventually, I managed to clear all the certification exams before the 6-month probation period. But I was physically and mentally exhausted. I did a lot of hard work. But I didn't get the required result. Later, I started pondering whether hard work is required for success.

I got the answer after watching the YouTube video of Vishen Lakhiani entitled 'The Lie Behind Working Hard For Success'. You can also watch this less than 5-minute video by clicking the following link:

https://youtu.be/_4q43bvDGP4

Vishen Lakhiani challenges the notion that "hard work" is the primary driver of success, arguing that while effort is important, it's not the only factor. He suggests that excessive work can lead to burnout and decreased productivity, and that a focus on mental well-being and strategic decision-making is equally, if not more, important.

***Here's a more detailed look at Lakhiani's perspective:***

- **The Productivity Curve:**

He points out that after a certain point, prolonged work hours lead to diminishing returns in productivity.

- **Cognitive Decline:**

Sleep deprivation and burnout can negatively impact cognitive abilities, making it harder to perform effectively.

- **Beyond Hard Work:**

Lakhiani emphasises the importance of mental clarity, emotional well-being, and strategic decision-making in achieving success.

- **Mindvalley's Approach:**

His company, Mindvalley, emphasises creating a positive and supportive work environment where employees can thrive, rather than solely relying on long hours.

- **The Importance of "Why":**

He highlights the significance of understanding one's motivations (happiness, money, mission, education) when choosing a career path, suggesting that aligning with core values is more effective than simply working hard.

I completely agree with Vishen Lakhiani. Our human body needs rest and recreation after doing work for a particular period. If we keep pushing ourselves after a particular period, we will invite boredom and inertia.

In my personal life, I make use of a famous time management technique invented by Francesco Cirillo, which is known as 'The Pomodoro Technique'.

The Pomodoro Technique is a time management method that uses a timer to break work into focused intervals, typically 25 minutes, with short breaks in between. Each focused work interval is called a "pomodoro". After four pomodoros, a longer break is taken.

*Here's how it works:*

1. **Choose a task:** Select the specific task or project you want to work on.
2. **Set the timer:** Start a timer for 25 minutes.
3. **Work without distractions:** Focus solely on the task until the timer goes off.
4. **Take a short break:** When the timer sounds, take a 5-minute break.
5. **Repeat:** Repeat the work and break cycle 3 more times.
6. **Take a longer break:** After four pomodoros, take a longer break (15-30 minutes).
7. **Repeat the process:** Start the cycle again with a new task or project.

*Why it works:*

- **Improves focus:** The structured intervals help maintain focus and reduce mental fatigue.
- **Minimises distractions:** The timer encourages you to avoid distractions and stay on task.
- **Prevents burnout:** Regular breaks prevent mental fatigue and burnout.
- **Boosts motivation:** The sense of accomplishment from completing a Pomodoro cycle can boost motivation.
- **Promotes accountability:** Tracking your Pomodoro sessions can help you stay accountable for your work.

Another time management technique which boosts productivity is time blocking. Time blocking is a time management technique where you schedule specific blocks of time for particular tasks. It involves dividing your day into segments, assigning each segment to a specific activity, and committing to working on that task during its designated time block. This method can help increase focus, reduce decision fatigue, and improve overall productivity.

***Here's a more detailed look at how time blocking works:***

1. Identify and Prioritise Tasks:
   - Create a list of tasks you need to complete.
   - Prioritise tasks based on urgency, importance, and your energy levels.
2. Estimate Time Requirements:
   - For each task, estimate how long it will take to complete.
   - Be realistic and avoid underestimating.
3. Block Out Time on Your Calendar:
   - Schedule specific blocks of time for each prioritised task.
   - Use a calendar app or digital planner to visually represent your time blocks.
4. Commit and Focus:
   - During each time block, focus solely on the assigned task and avoid multitasking.
   - Minimise distractions like social media and emails.
5. Review and Adjust:
   - At the end of each day or week, review your time blocks and assess their effectiveness.
   - Adjust your time blocks as needed based on your experience and changing priorities.

***Benefits of Time Blocking:***

- **Increased Focus:**

By dedicating specific time slots to tasks, you can avoid multitasking and maintain focus on one task at a time.

- **Reduced Decision Fatigue:**

Planning your day in advance can reduce the need to constantly decide what to work on next, which can be mentally draining.

- **Improved Time Management:**

Time blocking can help you better understand how you spend your time and identify areas where you can improve your efficiency.

- **Increased Productivity:**

By prioritising tasks and dedicating focused time to them, you can complete more work in less time.

- **Greater Work-Life Balance:**

By scheduling time for tasks and breaks, you can create a more balanced and fulfilling work-life experience.

- **Better Planning:**

Time blocking forces you to think about how long tasks will take, which can help you create more realistic estimates and plan your week effectively.

Before we commence our work, it is highly recommended to do at least half an hour of meditation. Meditation can boost productivity by enhancing focus, reducing stress, and improving cognitive function. Regular meditation practice can lead to increased concentration, mental clarity, and better time management, ultimately contributing to greater efficiency and effectiveness at work.

### *Here's how meditation can boost productivity:*

- **Increased Focus and Concentration:**

Meditation helps train the mind to focus and stay present, reducing distractions and improving the ability to concentrate on tasks.

- **Stress Reduction:**

By calming the mind and body, meditation can lower stress levels, which can otherwise hinder productivity and lead to burnout.

- **Improved Cognitive Function:**

Meditation can enhance cognitive flexibility and attention control, making it easier to switch between tasks and manage complex information.

- **Better Time Management:**

By reducing distractions and improving focus, meditation can help individuals manage their time more effectively and complete tasks more quickly.

- **Enhanced Emotional Regulation:**

Meditation can improve emotional regulation, allowing individuals to handle stressful situations with greater composure and resilience.

- **Increased Creativity:**

Quieting the mind through meditation can open up space for new ideas and creative problem-solving.

By following these techniques, we can boost our productivity. No matter how productive we are, we must never neglect our sleep. We need at least 8 hours of sleep every single day. I will talk about the importance of sleep in the next chapter.

# 5

# Importance of Sleep

**AN AVERAGE HUMAN** spends one-third of their lifetime sleeping. Sleep is an important aspect of human life, yet we take it for granted. Sleep is crucial for overall health and well-being, impacting physical and mental functions. It's vital for body repair, memory consolidation, immune system strength, and maintaining a healthy weight. Adequate sleep reduces stress, improves mood, and lowers the risk of chronic diseases like diabetes and heart disease.

We require at least 8 hours of sleep every single day. Anything less than 6 hours of sleep is an invitation to serious health problems like daytime sleepiness, impaired cognitive function, high blood pressure, obesity, heart disease, and stroke. Sleep deprivation can negatively impact how the body processes sugar, increasing the risk of developing type 2 diabetes. Lack of sleep can disrupt hormones that regulate appetite and metabolism, potentially leading to weight gain.

Arianna Huffington fainted from sleep deprivation and exhaustion, hit her head on her desk and broke her cheekbone. She now advocates for prioritising sleep, emphasising its crucial role in well-being, productivity, and overall life success. She believes that sleep is not a luxury but a necessity and has written a book, "The Sleep Revolution," exploring its impact on health and decision-making. Huffington encourages a "sleep revolution" to counter the cultural dismissal of sleep, highlighting the negative consequences of sleep deprivation.

In today's world, we sacrifice sleep for the sole purpose of realising our dreams and ambitions. Glamourising overwork and compromising sleep is applauded by many people. In the pursuit of professional excellence, people tend to overwork. Young people spend the late hours of the night watching movies on Netflix and eating unhealthy snacks.

Sleep should not be considered a waste of time and must receive the same importance as proper nutrition and exercise for maintaining health. Hard work is encouraged to achieve success in every field, but not at the cost of sleep.

***I would like to share a few guidelines that will help you to prioritise sleep.***

1. No electronic device at least 30 minutes before bedtime. Electronic devices emit blue light, which disrupts the production of Melatonin. Melatonin is a natural hormone which regulates the sleep-wake cycle and helps you fall asleep.
2. Avoid caffeine before going to sleep. Caffeine hinders our ability to fall asleep at night.
3. Keep your bedroom cool, quiet, and dark. To keep your bedroom cool at night, consider opening windows for cross-ventilation, using a fan to circulate air, and closing curtains or blinds during the day to block sunlight.
4. Meditation before bed can help improve sleep by calming the mind and body, making it easier to fall asleep and stay asleep.

***Benefits of Meditation for Sleep:***

- **Reduces Stress and Anxiety:** Meditation can help calm the mind and body, reducing stress and anxiety that can interfere with sleep.

- **Improves Sleep Quality:** Regular meditation practice can lead to deeper and more restful sleep.
- **May Help with Insomnia:** Meditation may be particularly helpful for individuals struggling with insomnia.
- **Encourages Relaxation:** Meditation promotes relaxation, which is essential for sleep.
- **Reduces Nighttime Wakings:** Some studies suggest that meditation can reduce the number of times you wake up during the night.

Matthew Walker is a British author, scientist and professor of neuroscience and psychology at the University of California, Berkeley. As an academic, Walker has focused on the impact of sleep on human health. He is considered to be the world's number one sleep expert. He wrote the book *Why We Sleep: The New Science of Sleep and Dreams* in 2017, which became a bestseller.

In the book, Walker discusses the importance of sleeping, the side effects of failing to do so, and its impact on society. Walker and his team spent roughly 20 years studying the rejuvenating ability of sleep. One particular research study was conducted where people volunteered to sleep for only six hours in a span of 10 nights. This resulted in the volunteers being "cognitively impaired" along with their brains being heavily damaged, regardless of the three-week, eight-hour sleep schedule they received later.

Walker wrote that research proves that sleeping after studying allows for "memory, integration and retention benefits" to occur. He further wrote that sleeping can help retain memories and enhance human learning abilities. Walker wrote the book in a "reader-friendly" way in areas such as discussing neuroscientific techniques and how they were created. The book ends with Walker's advice for better sleep through 12 tips, with one of them being to have a single eight-to-nine-hour period of sleep.

## *12 Tips for Healthy Sleep from Matthew Walker:*

**1. Stick to a Sleep Schedule:**

Go to bed and wake up at the same time each day, even on weekends, to regulate your body's natural sleep-wake cycle.

**2. Exercise Regularly, but Not Too Late:**

Aim for 30 minutes of daily exercise, but avoid intense workouts within 2-3 hours of bedtime.

**3. Limit Caffeine and Nicotine:**

Be mindful of your intake of coffee, tea, soda, and nicotine, as these substances can interfere with sleep.

**4. Avoid Alcohol Before Bed:**

While alcohol may initially induce drowsiness, it can disrupt REM sleep and negatively impact sleep quality.

**5. Avoid Large Meals and Beverages Late at Night:**

Indigestion and frequent awakenings to urinate can disrupt sleep, so opt for light meals and avoid large beverages before bed.

**6. Talk to Your Doctor About Medications:**

Discuss any medications that may be affecting your sleep with your doctor and explore alternative options, if possible.

**7. Avoid Napping After 3 PM:**

Naps can disrupt your natural sleep cycle, especially if taken too close to bedtime.

**8. Create a Relaxing Bedtime Routine:**

Incorporate relaxing activities into your evening routine to help you wind down and prepare for sleep.

**9. Take a Hot Bath or Shower Before Bed:**

The drop in body temperature after a warm bath can signal to your body that it's time to sleep.

**10. Optimise Your Sleep Environment:**

Ensure your bedroom is dark, cool (65-68°F), and quiet to promote restful sleep.

**11. Get Sunlight Exposure:**

Morning sunlight helps regulate your circadian rhythm and can improve sleep quality.

**12. Don't Lie in Bed Awake:**

If you find yourself staying awake for more than 20 minutes, then do some relaxing activity until you feel sleepy.

# 6

# What Vipassana Taught Me

**ON 30TH MAY** 2012, I went to Dhamma Giri to do the Vipassana Meditation Course for 10 days. I reached Dhamma Giri by the afternoon and was inquisitively looking at the beautiful place of the Vipassana Centre, which is situated at Igatpuri District in the state of Maharashtra.

After completing all the formalities, we were asked to submit any valuables to their office. I submitted Rs. 300, which was kept inside a sealed cover at their counter. Then we were allotted a specific room. I got a small room consisting of 2 beds, one table and a bathroom cum toilet. My room number was O-23. I had a roommate with whom I had to live for the next 10 days.

There are certain rules and regulations which we have to abide by if we are to become successful in Vipassana Meditation. The most important rule is that we are supposed to follow complete silence. We are not supposed to talk with any of the other Vipassana meditators. We cannot communicate with others even through gestures. However, we can discuss our meditation issues with our concerned teacher. Also, if there are any personal problems, we can discuss them with the management, who are referred to as 'Dhamma Sevaks'.

We were led to the meditation hall, where there were many meditation seats spread on the ground. Everyone got their respective seats and was told to attach a card on which our name, room number and group number were written inside a plastic cover, which is attached to the seat with the help of a safety pin. For all 10 days, we are supposed to do our meditation only on the seat which is assigned to us.

On 31st May 2012, the Vipassana Meditation started. We all got up at 4.00 am sharp and after brushing our teeth, we started our meditation by 4:30 am. We were asked to observe our breathing. This kind of meditation is termed 'Anapanasati'. We are not supposed to regulate our breath, like we do in Pranayama. We should just concentrate on natural breathing. At times, we are also suggested that if we cannot feel our breathing, then we can take a few deep breaths to feel our breathing and then come back to the natural flow of breathing. According to tradition, 'Anapanasati' was originally taught by the Buddha in several sutras, including the Anapanasati Sutta.

For successful Vipassana meditation, we also need to follow the 5 principles, which are termed as 'panchasheelas'. And these 'panchasheelas' are:

1. No killing.
2. No stealing.
3. No sexual misconduct.
4. No lying.
5. No intoxicants.

If you break any one of the sheelas, your mind is bound to get agitated, and you cannot make progress in Vipassana meditation.

For 3 days, we are supposed to practice only 'Anapanasati' meditation. In the initial phase, I experienced a lot of problems. I couldn't sit for 1 hour at a stretch. I used to get up from my meditation seat and go to the washroom for personal reasons. My teacher noticed this and advised me not to leave my meditation seat after every 20 minutes, which I used to do in my initial phase of meditation.

There are basically 3 main group meditation sittings. One group sitting was from 8 to 9 am. Another group sitting was from

2.30 to 3.30 pm, and the last one was from 6 to 7 pm. Our breakfast timing was from 6.30 to 7.15 am. Lunch time was from 11 to 11.45 am, and tea time was from 5 to 5.30 pm.

In the Vipassana Centre, food as well as accommodation are provided free of cost. However, at the end of the course, if we wish, we can give voluntary donations in the office, which will be used to help future students.

The Vipassana meditation gets completed at 9.30 pm, and we can retire to our respective residences for sleep. Laundry service is also available in the Vipassana Centre, where we can give our clothes for washing and ironing on a nominal charge of Rs. 7 per item. Laundry service will be available till 7.45 am only. We get the washed and ironed clothes the next morning.

Every day at 7.15 pm sharp, there is a discourse on Vipassana by Goenkaji. It is a wonderful video discourse on a projector where our Pujya Guruji gives specific guidance on Vipassana meditation. He talks on the "dos and don'ts" of Vipassana meditation and often explains them with the help of good stories, which are very relevant to the topic at hand. At times, he also uses humour, and it keeps the complications of the technique at bay, making the discourse enjoyable.

Meditation session gets ended with specific chanting in Pali, followed by chanting of a Buddhist mantra "Bhavatu Sabba Mangalam" 3 times. It means "May all beings be happy". All the meditators acknowledge the mantra by chanting "Sadhu" 3 times. This is the general practice of ending the meditation session.

Apart from the meditation hall, there is also a Pagoda cell in the Vipassana Centre. A pagoda is a tiered tower with multiple eaves. Initially, we were not allowed to enter the Pagoda cell. I got a chance to enter the Pagoda cell on my 7th day of the Vipassana course with the permission of my teacher. Inside the Pagoda, there are many individual cells. Inside every individual cell, there is an individual meditation seat which is spread on the ground. The cell is only for one meditator. There should be complete silence, and we can practice our Vipassana meditation inside the cell.

During group meditations, we are not supposed to enter the Pagoda for meditation. For group sittings, we should be available in the meditation hall.

The real Vipassana meditation started on the 4th day. We were given full instructions on the Vipassana technique for a complete 2 hours. We were told to feel the sensations of our body starting from the top of our head and moving down, and feeling sensations on our face, ears, throat, chest, hands, stomach, legs and finally feel sensations on the tip of our toes. Then we have to reverse the operation and start feeling sensations starting from the tip of our toes and moving up till we reach the top of our head and start feeling sensations there.

There would be times when you start feeling pleasant sensations, and there would be times when you feel unpleasant sensations. Sensations can be of any type. It can be heat, cold, a tingling sensation, a vibrating sensation, a prickling sensation, a tickling sensation, or it could be the sensation arising from the touch of the atmosphere on our body.

At times, we may feel some sensation in the form of discomfort arising because of keeping our body still for a long period of time. Whatever sensation we feel, we must keep in mind that they are all ephemeral or evanescent by nature and should not develop any kind of craving or aversion towards any kind of sensation.

Generally, when we feel some pleasant sensations in our body, we start developing a craving for that particular sensation, and it becomes our Samskara. But a wise man always knows that these sensations are short-lived and takes an effort never to form any kind of craving towards a pleasant sensation.

Similar is the case with unpleasant sensations. When we start feeling unpleasant sensations, we form an aversion towards them, and it becomes our Samskara. Again, a wise man knows that it is also a passing phase and should view even the unpleasant sensations with equanimity and a balanced mind.

This is what Vipassana teaches us – to view all the experiences of life with equanimity, knowing that it is all the passing phases of life, and one should not develop any kind of attachment in the form of aversion or craving.

When we start doing Vipassana Meditation, what happens is that our deep-rooted Samskaras come alive, and when we keep developing equanimity, these subtle Samskaras tend to slowly get removed from our mind, and we start experiencing true inner peace of mind.

This is the technique to eradicate the deep-rooted complexes of our mind, which keep manifesting as desires in the form of aversion or craving. These aversions and cravings have a tendency to get multiplied, and the more fuel we add to them, the more they keep multiplying till they take hold of the innermost recesses of our subconscious mind. When we don't react to those sensations, the feelings of aversion and craving don't get generated, and our mind becomes equanimous and balanced.

This is the theoretical aspect of Vipassana Meditation. As far as practice is concerned, we have to practice this meditation by keeping our bodies as still as possible. And then only we will be able to feel the subtle sensations on our body. We have to take a strong determination to maintain the same meditational posture throughout the one hour of our meditation. This is known as Addhithana. The practice is not as easy as it appears.

Initially, we may not be able to keep Addhithana. We keep changing our postures due to some discomfort. But as we keep practising, keeping a balanced mind throughout one hour of meditation, we will be able to keep Addhithana and become a successful Vipassana meditator.

Now I want to talk about our Vipassana teachers. There were 3 Vipassana teachers. My concerned teacher, with whom I can discuss my meditation issues, is Guruji Sandeep Shetty. He is a proficient Vipassana teacher who is highly observant of the students. He took utmost care to help the students overcome their difficulties in meditation.

There is always a meditation session for a small group, along with the teacher. All the meditators were distributed into various small groups consisting of some 10-12 students. I was in group number 18. And I, along with my other group mates, used to have a short meditation session with our Guruji. Our Guruji used to talk about the correct method of doing Vipassana meditation.

Guruji Sandeep Shetty used to be very observant on me. He noticed my shortcomings in meditation and used to discuss them privately with me at 7 pm. During the initial phase, my meditation session used to be on a very low profile. I used to get up after every 20 minutes to relieve myself from the excruciating discomfort which I often experience during the meditation session. My Guruji advised me not to interrupt the meditation in between and develop a strong determination to remain in the meditation session for one hour. Eventually, I learnt to prolong my meditation and remain in my meditational seat for one hour continuously.

At another point, I often used to make some facial expressions while doing meditation. Whenever I sit for meditation, many of my past negativities crop up in my mind and create some turbulence in my internal dialogue. Guruji Sandeep Shetty noticed this and explained to me about the ephemeral nature of the past Sanskaras. He told me to avoid all facial expressions and not to react to past negativities. He explained to me the ephemeral nature of the mind and told me to remain equanimous towards these negativities, which disturb the mind. He told me to keep my body as still as possible and concentrate on the sensations of my body. Through this practice, I soon overcame all my strong reactions towards the disturbing thoughts, and eventually I was able to avoid all the unwanted facial expressions which I used to make out of habit.

Guruji noticed my progress and told me that I had really learnt to keep my body still and that I don't make facial expressions anymore. I felt very happy about my progress. After doing Vipassana, I always felt greater joy and peace of mind. I always felt relief from the negativities of my past and found my mind becoming more stable, more peaceful and more concentrated.

After 5 or 6 days, my roommate got shifted to another room for some reason. My Guruji asked me whether I would be able to stay alone or will I would need any Dhamma Sevak to come to my residence to stay with me. I preferred to stay alone. I told my Guruji that I am quite confident to stay alone and told him that if I have any difficulty, then I will surely inform him. He permitted me to stay alone in my residence.

On the 10th day, we were allowed to break our Noble Silence and got the opportunity to interact with other Vipassana meditators. Before we could break our silence, we had to perform a special type of meditation known as Metta Bhavana, which means Loving-kindness meditation.

It is a meditation where a specific chant is done to show our gratitude and love towards all living beings. It is a short meditation where we share our inner virtues with others. But we are not supposed to chant along with the teacher. After Metta Bhavana Meditation, we are free to interact with others.

I made a couple of friends in the Vipassana Centre. Some of them are now my Facebook friends. Some of my friends were doctors, students, engineers or teachers. Most of them had experienced some or other trials and tribulations in their life.

Most of them had a purpose. The purpose is to free oneself from all the bondages and miseries which keep holding one back from realising the true joy of life. One of my friends was a drug addict. During the 10-day Vipassana Course, he found that he was able to keep his passions in check. He found better control over his emotions and passions.

On the last day, we were allowed to go up the stairs of the Pagoda cell. I found that on the top floor, there were various cells for meditation. But the cells were a little wider and more ventilated.

On the last day, the Vipassana book store was open for us, and students were allowed to purchase books. I brought 4 books on Vipassana and 2 video and audio CDS of Vipassana.

On the 11th day, i.e., on 10th June 2012, everyone bid goodbye to each other and we all returned to our respective homes. We all felt very happy and peaceful. Vipassana has given a new outlook towards our life.

I wish everyone gets inspired to join the Vipassana course and relieve oneself from all the impurities of the mind, which is the cause of all our miseries. May all beings be happy! "Bhavatu Sabba Mangalam!"

# 7

# Power of Sex Transmutation

**SEX TRANSMUTATION**, as discussed by Napoleon Hill in "Think and Grow Rich," refers to the redirection of sexual energy into other, more beneficial pursuits. It's not about eliminating sexual desire, but about channelling that energy toward creative endeavours, professional achievements, or personal growth. The core concept is that sexual thoughts and energy can be diverted to fuel other areas of life, leading to increased focus, drive, and success.

Celibacy is highly indispensable for our spiritual development. Celibacy is not the suppression of sex. It is the sublimation of sex. I have followed the path of sexual continence in my own life, and I have realised that without conserving our sexual energies, we cannot have real spiritual progress.

But suppression of sex is unhealthy. The suppression of sexuality can have negative consequences, including feelings of guilt, shame, anxiety, and even physical health problems. Suppressing sexual desires can create distance in relationships, leading to conflict and dissatisfaction.

When our mind is directed towards our goal, we have no time to indulge in cheap thrills and entertainment. Our whole day is spent learning new skills and upgrading ourselves. When we start conserving our sexual energies, the energy previously directed towards that area can be redirected towards other pursuits, such as spiritual growth, personal development, or creative endeavours.

Celibacy generally requires a significant amount of willpower and self-discipline. It involves consciously choosing to abstain from sexual activity, which can be a challenging decision for many individuals. The level of willpower needed depends on the individual's personal motivations, relationship dynamics, and the intensity of their sexual desires.

I idolise Swami Vivekananda. I was quite captivated by his oratory skills and personal magnetism. When I studied his life, I realised that he was a strict celibate. He was a Brahmachari. When Swami Vivekananda began his speech at the Parliament of the World's Religions in 1893 with the words "Sisters and Brothers of America," the entire audience of 7,000 people stood up and gave him a standing ovation. This ovation lasted for a few minutes, reflecting the audience's immediate and profound response to his welcoming words. Such is the power of celibacy!

I would like to highlight a few quotes of Swami Vivekananda on Brahmacharya:

*By the establishment of continence, energy is gained. The chaste brain has tremendous energy and gigantic willpower. Without chastity, there can be no spiritual strength. Continence gives wonderful control over mankind. The spiritual leaders of men have been very continent, and this is what gave them power. Therefore, the Yogi must be continent.*

*Complete continence gives great intellectual and spiritual power. The Brahmachârin must be sexually pure in thought, word, and deed. Lose regard for the body; get rid of the consciousness of it so far as possible.*

*In order to attain to ideal Brahmacharya, one has in the beginning to observe strict rules regarding chastity. Not only should one keep oneself strictly aloof from the least association with the opposite sex, but also give up the company of married people even.*

*The Sanskrit name for a student, Brahmachârin, is synonymous with the Sanskrit word Kâmajit. Our goal of life is Moksha; how can that be ever attained without Brahmacharya or absolute continence? Hence, it is imposed upon our boys and youth as an indispensable condition during their studentship. The purpose of life in the West is Bhoga, enjoyment; hence, much attention to strict Brahmacharya is not so indispensably necessary with them as it is with us.*

*You now have to make the character of Mahavira your ideal. See how, at the command of Ramachandra, he crossed the ocean. He had no care for life or death! He was a perfect master of his senses and wonderfully sagacious. You now have to build your life on this great ideal of personal service. Through that, all other ideals will gradually manifest in life. Obedience to the Guru without questioning, and strict observance of Brahmacharya – this is the secret of success.*

*Simply by the observance of strict Brahmacharya (continence), all learning can be mastered in a very short time – one has an unfailing memory of what one hears or knows but once. It is owing to this want of continence that everything is on the brink of ruin in our country.*

Practising absolute Brahmacharya (celibacy) for 12 years is believed to bring about significant spiritual and physical benefits, including the opening of the Medha Nadi (intelligence nerve), strong memory, heightened awareness, and the realisation of God. It is also thought to lead to a state of Samadhi (deep meditative state) without effort and to facilitate the development of a strong will and healthy body.

But it is not so easy to follow the path of Brahmacharya. God has made sexual desire very powerful, keeping in view the continuity of the human race. There are so many hurdles in the path of celibacy. If you are interested in following this great path, then I highly recommend that you read the book entitled '*Practice of Brahmacharya*' written by Swami Sivananda.

This book deals with the vital subject of Brahmacharya in a forceful, but homely style, and prescribes potent means and methods for the eradication of lust, sublimation of sex-energy into Ojas shakti for attaining the goal of life – God-realization.

*Here are some key highlights from the book:*

- **Brahmacharya as a path to spiritual advancement:**

The book emphasises that Brahmacharya is a crucial practice for achieving spiritual liberation and self-realisation.

- **Techniques for controlling desires:**

Swami Sivananda outlines various methods for controlling the senses, including fasting, dietary restrictions, Pranayama, Japa, meditation, and thought control.

- **Importance of Vichara (enquiry):**

The book encourages the practice of the "Who am I?" enquiry to overcome the influence of old samskaras and vasanas (mental impressions).

- **Transmuting lust into Ojas shakti:**

"Practice of Brahmacharya" emphasises the ability to transform lustful energy into divine energy, which is essential for spiritual progress.

- **The benefits of Brahmacharya:**

The book highlights the benefits of Brahmacharya, including a strong, healthy body, a sharp mind, increased willpower, and a charming personality.

- **Practical guidance for different life stages:**

The book guides students, married couples, and renunciates, emphasising the importance of self-control and regulated sex life where celibacy is not possible.

With this, I end this chapter. In the next chapter, I will talk about the power of silence. Happy Reading!

# 8

# Power of Silence

**SILENCE IS OFTEN** underestimated, yet it holds significant power for personal growth, clarity, and better communication. In a world filled with noise and distractions, silence allows for reflection, introspection, and a deeper connection with oneself and others.

Silence offers numerous benefits, including stress reduction, improved focus, enhanced creativity, and better sleep. It can also promote mindfulness, self-awareness, and improved relationships. Silence helps calm racing thoughts, stimulates brain growth, and encourages deeper reflection.

I spend most of my time in silence. During this period, I read a nonfiction book (I don't read fiction) or meditate. Silence is a key practice for awakening the Law of Pure Potentiality, the first of Deepak Chopra's Seven Spiritual Laws of Success. By creating space for silence and stillness, you can access a state of being where you can connect with your true nature and tap into the boundless potential within.

Silence plays an important role in Buddhism. Noble Silence (Samatha) in Buddhism refers to a period of abstaining from all communication, including speech, gestures, and writing, for a specific duration, often during retreats or meditation practices. It's also attributed to the Buddha, who reportedly chose silence in response to certain unanswerable questions about ultimate reality.

Observing noble silence in meditation, which involves both the silence of speech and thought, helps cultivate tranquillity, self-awareness, and a deeper understanding of the nature of reality. It allows thoughts and emotions to surface and be observed without attachment or judgment, leading to a clearer view of oneself and the world.

In various spiritual traditions, silence is seen as a way to connect with the divine, whether it be through meditation, prayer, or simply quiet contemplation. By silencing the mind, one can better hear the inner voice or guidance from a higher power.

Silence encourages a greater awareness of the present moment, fostering a sense of connection to oneself and the world around. It helps to cultivate mindfulness, allowing individuals to be more present in their daily lives.

Silence can help to calm the mind and body, reducing stress and anxiety. It provides a respite from the constant stimulation of modern life, allowing individuals to experience a deeper sense of inner peace and tranquillity.

Silence can sharpen intuition, allowing individuals to access their inner wisdom and guidance. By creating a space for quiet contemplation, one can better discern their true intentions and values.

Silence can provide a space for healing and transformation, allowing individuals to work through emotional wounds and past traumas. It can also help to cultivate a more compassionate and understanding heart.

Silence can spark creativity and innovation, allowing individuals to tap into their inner wellspring of ideas and inspiration. It can also help to foster a more imaginative and playful approach to life.

Despite the benefits of silence, it can also have some adverse effects, especially when it's a forced silence or used as a form of punishment or emotional abuse. In such cases, silence can lead to feelings of isolation, anxiety, and depression, as well as hinder communication and healthy relationship dynamics.

When individuals are silenced or pressured to remain silent, it can prevent them from expressing their feelings, needs, and experiences, leading to a build-up of negative emotions and stress. Silence can create a sense of isolation and loneliness, especially when it's a result of being excluded or not having an opportunity to connect with others. The inability to express oneself and the constant pressure to remain silent can trigger the stress response in the body, leading to a range of physical and mental health issues.

And that is the main reason why we must never practise Vipassana meditation just by reading books. Vipassana meditation, while beneficial for many, is not recommended for individuals with serious mental health conditions. The intense focus and discipline required can exacerbate existing mental health issues, and the strict rules of the retreats may not be conducive to individuals with unstable interpersonal relationships or a history of various treatments. Additionally, the prolonged periods of silence and detachment from external stimuli can be challenging for some individuals.

Deepak Chopra emphasises that silence is a profound state, not just the absence of sound, but a presence of inner stillness and awareness. He suggests it's a gateway to spiritual intelligence, connecting us to our deepest essence and allowing us to access wisdom beyond ordinary thought. Practising silence through techniques like meditation can help us experience this inner silence and tap into our source of peace and clarity.

Silence and solitude can be a powerful catalyst for creativity. Without the distractions of the outside world, you're free to let your mind wander and explore new ideas. Many famous creatives, from Albert Einstein to Stephen King, have credited silence and solitude with helping them tap into their creative potential.

Silence can play a significant role in achieving Vak Siddhi (the power of articulate and effective speech), according to some spiritual traditions. By practising silence, particularly within oneself, one can purify the mind and body, leading to a more refined and powerful ability to speak.

While silence is a powerful tool, it's important to note that Vak Siddhi can also be achieved through other practices like mantra chanting, yoga, and meditation. The specific path and methods may vary depending on individual needs and inclinations.

*Achieving progressive control over the organs of speech, body, and mind is Maun (silence). According to the Path of Devotion (Bhakti Marg), 'forgetting to speak as a result of remaining engrossed in contemplation of God', is the real silence.*

# 9

# Importance of Me Time

**I AM AN** introvert. I love solitude. It is not that I am antisocial, but I find solitude more comfortable than being in company. While I am in solitude, I find my creativity at its peak. My concentration level is high during these moments of stillness. In this chapter, I will elucidate the importance of 'Me Time'.

'Me Time' is the conscious effort of recharging your inner batteries amid the hustle and bustle of life. It can be achieved by reading a good book, doing meditation, performing yoga, and indulging in spiritual retreats. It can be done by walking barefoot on the grass. This practice is known as grounding, and it offers innumerable benefits to our body. It can help with stress reduction, improved sleep, enhanced immune function, pain relief, and better circulation.

At present, we think that spending time on ourselves is a waste of time. We believe that we must always be involved in various activities during our waking hours. We believe that 'being busy' is the sign of a successful person. This perception must be changed.

In Stephen Covey's bestselling book '*The 7 Habits of Highly Effective People*', he talks about the four quadrants of time management.

Quadrant 1: Urgent and important.

Quadrant 2: Not urgent yet important.

Quadrant 3: Urgent but not important.

Quadrant 4: Not urgent and not important.

The Four Quadrants model categorises each task, responsibility or relationship based on its urgency and importance. The objective of using this model is to improve both your personal and professional relationships and promote growth and accomplishment.

Most people in today's world spend maximum time in Quadrant 3. This is the quadrant of distraction, all those urgent matters that come to your attention that you shouldn't be dealing with. These could include useless phone calls, interruptions, some emails that you shouldn't be responding to, and meetings that don't achieve anything. These tasks tend to hijack your time away from the important matters of your day.

If you want to be truly successful, then you need to spend maximum time in Quadrant 2 (Not urgent yet important). Reading a book may not be urgent, but it is important if you want to enhance your knowledge. Walking barefoot on grass is not urgent, but this practice offers innumerable benefits to our bodies. Doing meditation may not be urgent, but it is important because it develops our intuition.

I would like to elucidate the innumerable benefits which 'Me Time' activities offer.

### *Benefits of Reading a Non-Fiction Book*

- **Improved Critical Thinking:**

Non-fiction requires readers to analyse information, identify key concepts, and draw conclusions, fostering critical thinking skills.

- **Expanded Knowledge and Understanding:**

Non-fiction exposes readers to new ideas, perspectives, and real-world situations, broadening their knowledge base and understanding of complex topics.

- **Enhanced Writing Skills:**

Reading well-written non-fiction can improve your writing abilities by demonstrating how to structure arguments, present information clearly, and use language effectively.

- **Increased Empathy:**

Non-fiction, particularly biographies and historical accounts, can provide insights into the lives and experiences of others, fostering empathy and understanding.

- **Improved Focus and Concentration:**

Engaging with complex non-fiction requires sustained attention and concentration, strengthening these cognitive skills.

- **Personal Growth and Inspiration:**

Non-fiction can be empowering by providing valuable life lessons, inspiring individuals to achieve their goals, and encouraging personal growth.

- **Better Communication Skills:**

Reading non-fiction, particularly on topics related to your interests or career, can improve your communication skills and make you a more knowledgeable and engaging conversationalist.

- **Enhanced Cognitive Function:**

Studies have shown that reading, including non-fiction, can improve memory, cognitive flexibility, and overall brain health.

- **Increased Awareness:**

Non-fiction can increase awareness of current events, global issues, and social problems, making readers more informed and engaged citizens.

- **Learning from Experts and Others:**

Non-fiction often provides insights from experts and individuals who have faced challenges and overcome obstacles, offering valuable lessons and inspiration.

- **Building Vocabulary and Language Skills:**

Non-fiction can introduce new words and phrases, expanding vocabulary and improving language skills.

- **Improved Awareness of the World:**

Non-fiction can help readers understand the world around them, including different cultures, histories, and perspectives.

- **Better Understanding of Reality:**

Non-fiction provides a deeper understanding of reality by exploring factual information and real-world events.

### *Benefits of Walking Barefoot on Grass*

- **Stress Reduction and Improved Sleep:**

Walking barefoot on grass can help balance the body's electrical charge, potentially reducing stress and improving sleep quality.

- **Improved Circulation:**

Grounding can improve blood flow, potentially benefiting cardiovascular health.

- **Pain Relief and Reduced Inflammation:**

The practice may help reduce pain and inflammation by neutralising harmful free radicals.

- **Enhanced Immunity:**

Walking barefoot on grass can stimulate the nervous system and improve the body's resilience.

- **Better Posture and Balance:**

Barefoot walking activates muscles in the feet and lower legs, which can improve posture and balance over time.

- **Improved Vision:**

Some believe that stimulating pressure points on the soles of the feet can energise the eyes and potentially improve vision.

### *Benefits of Regular Meditation*

1. Mental and Emotional Benefits:

- **Stress and Anxiety Reduction:**

Meditation helps calm the nervous system, lowering stress hormones and promoting relaxation.

- **Improved Emotional Well-being:**

Regular practice can lead to increased self-awareness, emotional regulation, and a greater sense of peace and contentment.

- **Enhanced Cognitive Abilities:**

Meditation can improve focus, concentration, and memory.

- **Increased Self-Awareness:**

Meditation can help you become more attuned to your thoughts and feelings, fostering self-understanding and personal growth.

2. Physical Benefits:

- **Boosted Immune System:**

Studies suggest that meditation can increase the production of immune cells and antibodies, enhancing your body's ability to fight off illness.

- **Improved Sleep:**

Meditation can help calm the mind and body, making it easier to fall asleep and improve sleep quality.

- **Reduced Pain:**

Meditation can help manage chronic pain by reducing muscle tension and promoting relaxation.

- **Lower Blood Pressure and Heart Rate:**

Regular meditation can lower resting heart rate and blood pressure, reducing strain on the heart and blood vessels.

3. Other Benefits:

- **Increased Creativity:**

By quieting the mind, meditation can free up mental space for creative thinking and problem-solving.

- **Enhanced Empathy and Compassion:**

Meditation can help you develop a greater understanding of yourself and others, fostering compassion and kindness.

- **Improved Emotional Stability:**

Meditation can help you manage emotional fluctuations, minimise mood swings, and develop emotional resilience.

- **Increased Willpower:**

Meditation can enhance mental discipline, making it easier to control impulses and overcome bad habits.

Indulging in 'Me Time' is indispensable if you want to lead a balanced life. Stop considering 'Me Time' as a waste of time and enjoy the innumerable benefits it offers.

# 10

# Become a Lifelong Learner

**LIFE IS ALL** about learning. It is a continuous process of acquiring knowledge, skills, and experiences. This perspective emphasises the idea that we are constantly evolving and growing, whether through formal education, self-directed learning, or simply observing the world around us. It highlights the importance of being open to new information, adapting to changes, and embracing new challenges.

I consider myself a lifelong learner. In 2024, I turned 41 years old. In this span of 41 years, I have learnt oratory, expert chess (I am still not a chess grandmaster), improved my lexicon, become an IELTS trainer and a Personality Development Coach and learnt 4 languages (English, Hindi, Malayalam and Marathi). I have also learnt a bit of Astrology, Palmistry and Numerology. I regularly read a non-fiction book and expand my erudition. I must have read at least more than 6000 books in 41 years.

My future goal is to learn foreign languages like French and Japanese. I want to learn the flute and become a professional flautist. I also want to become a chess grandmaster. I want to learn all the difficult words of the English language (I idolise Shashi Tharoor for his incredible vocabulary).

I read only non-fiction books like self-help, biographies and autobiographies, spiritual, health, business, psychology and other non-fiction books. I have read only one book based on fiction. And the name of that book is 'The Alchemist', written by Paulo Coelho. I believe that reading books based on fiction is a waste of time because we don't get much knowledge from reading such books. We only get entertainment and a vivid sense of imagination by reading fiction.

I have read hundreds of biographies and autobiographies. I have read the biography of Swami Vivekananda, A.P.J. Abdul Kalam, Paramahamsa Yogananda, Oprah Winfrey, Elon Musk, Om Swami, Indira Gandhi, Ratan Tata, Albert Einstein and other great personalities. I realise that reading biographies gives you a broader perspective on life. You learn about their life journey. You learn about their difficulties and challenges, and how they faced those challenges. This gives you the necessary strength to face your trials and tribulations of life. This turns you more resilient and perseverant.

The concept of lifelong learning recognises that learning doesn't stop after formal education. It encompasses continuous self-improvement and personal development throughout our lives. Most people stop learning once they have completed their school or college education. They secure a 9-to-5 job where the only focus is to get a monthly salary and pay the bills. They wait for the weekend so that they can go to the movies or spend time in Pizza Hut gourmandising on the pizza.

To become a lifelong learner, cultivate curiosity, embrace challenges, and continuously seek knowledge and skills. This involves adopting a growth mindset, actively seeking new experiences, and using technology to enhance learning. A growth mindset is the belief that intelligence, abilities, and talents are not fixed but can be developed through dedication, effort, and learning. It involves viewing challenges and setbacks as opportunities to learn and grow, and a belief that success is attainable through consistent effort.

Lifelong learning offers numerous benefits, enhancing individual and societal well-being. It leads to improved cognitive function, increased self-confidence, and career advancement, while also fostering adaptability and personal growth. Continuous learning can also improve social connections and mental health, ultimately leading to a more fulfilling and enriched life.

***Here's a more detailed look at the benefits:***

1. Personal Development:
   - **Cognitive Improvement:**

   Learning new things keeps the brain active and engaged, which can improve cognitive function and potentially delay cognitive decline.
   - **Increased Self-Confidence:**

   Successfully mastering new skills and knowledge can boost self-esteem and confidence.
   - **Personal Fulfilment:**

   Pursuing lifelong learning can be a source of joy and satisfaction, allowing individuals to explore their interests and passions.
   - **Enhanced Social Connections:**

   Engaging in learning opportunities can lead to meeting new people and building social networks.
2. Career Advancement:
   - **Adaptability and Resilience:**

   In a rapidly changing world, lifelong learners are better equipped to adapt to new challenges and changes in the workplace.
   - **Increased Job Security:**

   Continuous learning and upskilling can improve job prospects and make individuals more competitive in the job market.
   - **Career Advancement:**

   Learning new skills and knowledge can open doors to promotions and other career opportunities.

3. Social and Economic Benefits:
   - **Increased Productivity:**

   Lifelong learning can lead to increased productivity and efficiency in the workplace.
   - **Economic Benefits:**

   Lifelong learning can contribute to economic growth by creating a more skilled and adaptable workforce.
   - **Active Citizenship:**

   Lifelong learning can empower individuals to become more active and engaged citizens.
   - **Social Inclusion:**

   Lifelong learning can help individuals from marginalised groups to gain access to education and training, fostering social inclusion.
4. Mental Health Benefits:
   - **Reduced Stress and Anxiety:** Learning new things can be a healthy way to reduce stress and anxiety.
   - **Improved Mental Well-being:** Engaging in lifelong learning can improve mental well-being and overall quality of life.

I would like to end this chapter with the Guru Mantra for Self-Improvement:

*Day By Day, In Every Way,*
*I Am Becoming Successful,*
*In Every Walk Of Life,*
*Happier, Healthier, Richer,*
*Better And Better!*

# 11

# Understanding Prakriti - Sattva, Rajas and Tamas

**IN SAMKHYA PHILOSOPHY**, Prakriti, which means "nature" or "original form," is understood as the source of all manifestation and is characterised by three fundamental qualities called gunas: Sattva, Rajas, and Tamas.

**Sattva (Goodness/Purity):**

Represents balance, harmony, wisdom, serenity, and a positive disposition conducive to spiritual growth. It is associated with clarity of thought, knowledge, and selfless service. In the Bhagavad Gita, actions performed in Sattva lead to pure results and spiritual upliftment.

**Rajas (Passion/Activity):**

Embodies passion, activity, and movement. It is associated with dynamism, ambition, and the pursuit of desires. Actions done in Rajas result in pain and attachment, often leading to a cycle of unfulfilled desires.

**Tamas (Ignorance/Inertia):**

Reflects darkness, inertia, and ignorance. It is associated with lethargy, rigidity, and delusion. Actions performed under the influence of Tamas result in darkness, delusion, and regression.

The three gunas affect us deeply. They influence everything about us, from our thoughts and actions to the habits and activities that make us who we are. This means that whichever guna is more present within you will affect how you perceive the world. For instance, a predominantly tamasic person will see everything as negative and destructive. A more Sattvic person, on the other hand, will have a positive outlook and find joy and happiness in everything.

"You are what you eat." It means that the quality of what we eat, digest, and absorb has a direct impact on how we look, feel, and think. This applies to the gunas as well. Ayurvedic diets encourage us to **eat highly nutritious sattvic foods, moderate rajasic foods and no tamasic foods**. By doing this, we can live a healthier and more balanced life, physically, emotionally, and spiritually.

### *Here is a list of foods that influence the three gunas:*

**Sattvic Foods**

To increase Sattva, eat fresh, whole and nutritious foods like:

- Legumes
- Wholegrains
- Vegetables and fruits that are grown in the sun

**Rajasic Foods**

To reduce Rajas, limit your intake of foods that are stimulating in nature. This includes:

- Spicy foods
- Chillies and peppers
- Vegetables like onions
- Stimulants such as caffeine
- Pulses and dals

**Tamasic Foods**

Foods that reflect lethargy are tamasic. To decrease Tamas, avoid the following:

- Fast foods

- Refined foods like white bread
- Frozen foods or leftovers
- Red meat such as lamb and beef
- Mouldy cheeses

The goal of human life is to transcend Rajas and Tamas and attain Sattva. But Sattva also binds you to this material world. Rajas and Tamas are like iron chains, and Sattva is like a golden chain. The ultimate goal of human life is to attain the state of Gunatita.

In the context of spirituality, particularly Advaita Vedanta, "Gunatita" signifies a state of transcendence, where an individual is liberated from the limitations of the three qualities (gunas) of nature, as well as any other attributes or characteristics.

### *Here's a more detailed explanation:*

1. **Transcendence of Qualities:**
    - The three gunas - sattva (goodness), rajas (passion), and tamas (ignorance) - are fundamental qualities that influence all things in the universe.
    - A Gunatita person is beyond these gunas and is not bound by them.
    - This state of being free from the gunas is achieved through dedicated spiritual practices and is considered a state of liberation.
2. **Liberation from Limitations:**
    - A Gunatita is not limited by any specific characteristic or quality.
    - This means they are not identified with their ego, desires, or any other personal attachments.
    - They have attained a state of pure awareness and understanding, where they are free from the limitations of the self.
3. **Spiritual Elevation and Connection with the Divine:**
    - Gunatita individuals are said to have direct visions of God, indicating a profound connection with the divine.

- Their spiritual elevation allows them to experience reality beyond the ordinary perception of the world.

4. **Beyond Dualities:**
   - A Gunatita transcends the dualities of existence, such as good and bad, right and wrong.
   - They see the underlying unity of reality and are free from the suffering caused by these dualities.
5. **Not a State of Mindlessness:**
   - It's important to note that being Gunatita does not mean a person is in a state of mindlessness.
   - Thoughts may still arise in their mind, but they are not bound by them, nor are they subject to the influence of the gunas.

In essence, Gunatita is a state of being beyond the limitations of the self and the world, a state of liberation, spiritual elevation, and a profound connection with the divine.

Before we can reach the state of Gunatita, we have to work on our Rajas and Tamas and attain the state of Sattva. In this Kaliyuga, there is a predominance of Rajas and Tamas. Hence, there is so much evil in this world. If we have to bring back peace in this world, then we have to cultivate Sattva in our human consciousness.

To balance rajas (activity, passion) and tamas (inertia, ignorance), aim for a state of sattva (balance, clarity, harmony). This can be achieved through lifestyle adjustments, mindful practices, and dietary choices.

1. **Balancing Rajas:**
   - **Reduce stimulating activities:**

Avoid excessive exercise, loud music, overthinking, and material possessions.

- **Prioritise relaxation:**

Incorporate gentle yoga, pranayama (breathing exercises), and mindful meditation.

- **Mindful eating:**

Opt for sattvic foods like fruits, vegetables, and whole grains, while avoiding spicy, fried, or processed foods.

- **Practice self-awareness:**

Recognise and respond to impulses instead of reacting immediately.

2. **Balancing Tamas:**
   - **Increase activity:** Engage in physical activities like walking, yoga, or gardening to stimulate the body and mind.
   - **Seek stimulating environments:** Surround yourself with positive people, bright lights, and engaging activities.
   - **Avoid inactivity:** Minimise TV watching, oversleeping, and other sedentary behaviours.
   - **Practice mindfulness:** Be present in the moment and engage with your surroundings.
   - **Choose sattvic foods:** Eat light and fresh foods like fruits, vegetables, and whole grains, while avoiding heavy, stale, or processed foods.
3. **Cultivating Sattva:**
   - **Practice yoga and meditation:** These practices promote balance and clarity.
   - **Engage in positive activities:** Spend time in nature, listen to uplifting music, and surround yourself with good company.
   - **Cultivate compassion and kindness:** Practice non-violence and empathy towards yourself and others.
   - **Prioritise self-care:** Get enough sleep, eat nutritious foods, and engage in activities that bring joy.

By making conscious choices in your daily life and practising mindful habits, you can gradually move towards a more balanced state of sattva, where rajas and tamas are in harmony.

# 12

# Law of Karma

**THE LAW OF** Karma is an ancient Indian concept that refers to an action, work, or deed and its effect or consequences. Good intent and good deeds contribute to good karma and happier rebirths, while bad intent and bad deeds contribute to bad karma and worse rebirths. The law of Karma is also known as the law of cause and effect.

I have experienced the working of this law in my own life. Whenever I generate any dislike or hatred towards someone, nature punishes me then and there by filling my whole being with negativity. On the other hand, when I send blessings and prayers to someone, I feel quite blissful, and I attract positive situations in my life. Whether you like it or not, whatever you are experiencing currently is the result of your past actions.

Whatever goes around comes around. If we know this subtle truth, we will never indulge in any sinful deeds. On the other hand, we will start practising good deeds in our day-to-day life. We will start emitting positive thought vibrations to this world. Whenever we see others succeeding, we feel happy for their success instead of feeling envious and emitting negative thought vibrations.

In today's world, people are constantly emitting negative thought vibrations. Even for petty matters, we fight with our fellow beings. We fight in the name of religion. We never contemplate the damage it causes to our physical and mental health. Research has proved that holding negative thoughts and emotions causes serious health problems, including high blood pressure, cardiovascular issues, and even digestive disorders.

On the other hand, when we practise silent prayers and fill our mind with gratitude, it elevates our consciousness, leading to improved physical and mental health. In life, we never get what we desire. We only get what we deserve. And we know what we deserve. If you have done adequate good karma in your life, then you truly deserve all the blessings of life.

In Hindu and Buddhist traditions, karma is categorised into four main types: Sanchita, Prarabdha, Agami, and Kriyamana (or Vartamana). These categories help understand how karma affects an individual's life and future.

### *Here's a breakdown of each type:*

- **Sanchita Karma:**

This is the accumulated karma from past actions across lifetimes, a vast storehouse of actions and reactions waiting to be experienced. It's the total karmic balance that has accumulated over time.

- **Prarabdha Karma:**

This is a portion of Sanchita karma that is currently bearing fruit and determining the circumstances of the present life. It's the karma that is "ripened" and causing the present life's experiences.

- **Agami Karma:**

This is future karma that is created by present actions. It's the karma that is being created in the present and will manifest in the future.

- **Kriyamana Karma (Vartamana Karma):**

This is the karma created by current actions, which may yield results in the present or future. It's the karma that is being created right now, and its results may be experienced immediately or later.

To break free from the cycle of karma, focus on self-reflection, mindfulness, compassion, and positive actions. Essentially, it's about understanding the consequences of your actions and choosing to act with greater awareness and intention, particularly focusing on actions that benefit both yourself and others.

*Breaking Free from the Karmic Cycle:*

- **Self-Reflection:**

Regularly assess your actions, intentions, and their consequences. Are your actions truly aligned with your values and the well-being of others?

- **Mindfulness:**

Practice being present in the moment, observing your thoughts and actions without judgment. This allows you to make more conscious choices.

- **Compassion:**

Cultivate empathy and kindness towards yourself and others. Understand that everyone is facing their challenges.

- **Positive Action:**

Engage in actions that benefit yourself and others. This includes acts of service, forgiveness, and cultivating positive relationships.

- **Forgiveness:**

Practice forgiveness of yourself and others. Holding onto resentment can create new karmic bonds.

- **Take Responsibility:**

Take ownership of your mistakes and learn from them. Don't repeat harmful patterns.

- **Nourish your Spirit:**

Engage in practices that connect you to something larger than yourself, such as meditation, prayer, or spending time in nature.

- **Chanting and Mantras:**

Some traditions use chanting mantras, like the Vajrasattva mantra, to purify negative karma.

- **Follow Ethical Guidelines:**

Many spiritual traditions, like Buddhism, offer guidelines for ethical living, such as the Four Noble Truths and the Eightfold Path, to help break free from suffering and negative karma.

The 100-syllable Vajrasattva mantra is a powerful Buddhist mantra used for purification and spiritual development. Vajrasattva, also called the Great Purifier, is one of the most powerful and profound healing and purification techniques in Vajrayana Buddhism. It's very blessing and powerful to eliminate heavy karma.

***Vajrasattva mantra:***

OM BENZAR SATU SAMAYA
MANU PALAYA
BENZAR SATU TE NOPA
TI TRA DRI DROH ME BHA WA
SU TO KA YO ME BHA WA
SU PO KA YO ME BHA WA
ANU RAKTO ME BHA WA
SARVA SIDDHI ME DRA YATSA
SARVA KARMA SU TSA ME
TSITTAM SHERI YAM KU RU HUNG
HA HA HA HA HO BHA GA WAN
SARVA TA THA GA TA BENZRA
MA ME MUNTSA BENZRI BHA WA
MA HA SAMAYA SATO AH

***Translation:***

OM Vajrasattva, protect the Samaya
May you remain firm in me
Grant me complete satisfaction
Grow within me (increase the positive within me)
Be loving towards me

Grant me all the siddhis
Show me all the karmas (activities)
Make my mind good, virtuous and auspicious!
O blessed one, who embodies all the Vajra Tathagatas
Do not abandon me
Grant me the realisation of the Vajra Nature
O great Samayasatva
Make me one with you

In Buddhist tradition, the mantra is chanted at least 21 times daily for the purification of the mind. It is said that the practice will free one of all negative karma and impure thoughts that keep passing our mind. The texts also emphasise pronunciation. Just like in the case of any other mantra, the right pronunciation of the Vajrasattva mantra is necessary for expected results.

You can listen to this chanting on YouTube by clicking on the following link:

https://www.youtube.com/watch?v=xirefZnlfkQ

***Key Benefits of the Vajrasattva Mantra:***

- **Purification of Negative Karma:**

The mantra is a primary tool for purifying negative actions, both past and present.

- **Preventing Future Negative Karma:**

Regularly reciting the mantra helps prevent the accumulation of new negative karma, making it a powerful method for preventing suffering.

- **Facilitating Spiritual Progress:**

By purifying negative karma and reducing obstacles, the mantra facilitates spiritual progress, making it easier to attain enlightenment.

- **Increasing Merit and Wisdom:**

Vajrasattva practice, including mantra recitation, helps build merit and develop spiritual insights, ultimately leading to greater wisdom.

- **Protection and Guidance:**

The mantra is believed to provide protection and guidance, especially during times of hardship or when facing challenges.

- **Preparing for Death:**

Vajrasattva practice helps prepare practitioners for death, ensuring a positive and auspicious rebirth.

- **Clarity of Mind and Peace:**

Regular practice can contribute to a clearer and calmer mind, fostering inner peace and well-being.

- **Increased Love and Compassion:**

The practice can deepen feelings of love, compassion, and kindness towards oneself and others.

- **Fostering Spiritual Connection:**

The mantra connects practitioners to Vajrasattva and the Buddha, fostering a sense of spiritual connection and guidance.

*"Plant seeds of happiness, hope, success, and love; it will all come back to you in abundance. This is the law of nature."*

**- Steve Maraboli**

# 13

# Staying Grounded

*"**ACCEPT WHERE YOU** Are to Get You Where You Want to Go. Seeing clearly, accepting, and starting where you are. Not where you want to be. Not where you think you should be. Not where other people think you should be. But where you are. Be Present So You Can Own Your Attention and Energy. Being present, both physically and mentally, for what is in front of you. Spending more time fully in this life, not in thoughts about the past or future."*

**- Brad Stulberg, *The Practice of Groundedness***

Staying grounded means maintaining emotional stability and a sense of being present in the current moment despite external stressors or internal turmoil. It involves being connected to one's core values, purpose, and vision for life rather than being controlled by chaos or external factors.

Groundedness is about developing resilience and strength by connecting with oneself, others, and the world around us, rather than constantly striving for peak performance and external validation. If you want to practise groundedness, you must implement the following six principles in your day-to-day life:

**1. Acceptance and Presence:** Learning to accept where you are in life, rather than constantly striving for a future state, is crucial for groundedness. This involves practising presence, being mindful of your surroundings, and owning your attention and energy.

**2. Patience and Perseverance:** Groundedness emphasises the importance of patience, recognising that genuine progress and growth often take time and consistent effort. It's about focusing on the journey rather than solely on the destination.

**3. Embracing Vulnerability:** Instead of fearing vulnerability, groundedness encourages individuals to embrace it as a source of strength and connection. This involves being open to sharing emotions and experiences and fostering authentic relationships.

**4. Building Deep Community:** Cultivating meaningful connections with others is a fundamental aspect of groundedness. This includes finding a sense of belonging, whether through personal relationships, shared interests, or community service.

**5. Movement and Physical Well-being:** Regular physical activity is essential for grounding the mind and body. This can include exercise, yoga, meditation, or any form of movement that connects you with your physical self.

**6. Focus on the Process:** Groundedness encourages individuals to focus on the present moment and the ongoing process of growth, rather than obsessing over outcomes or striving for perfection.

In today's world, it can feel that if you want to be successful, you must constantly "hustle" and relentlessly pursue self-improvement. In *The Practice of Groundedness*, Brad Stulberg argues that many of us have fallen prey to this culture of productivity that glorifies working hard, staying busy, and chasing success above all else. But instead of feeling satisfied with our lives, we experience burnout, illness, and unhappiness.

Stulberg writes that, in today's world, **we obsess over ways to increase productivity and maximise efficiency, often at the expense of our well-being.** Society floods us with messages pushing us to improve how we live and work, and technology has furthered this culture of busyness—smartphone apps, for instance, allow us to track everything from our productivity to the calories we burn during a workout. Because of this, we often find ourselves on a never-ending quest for peak performance and greater happiness.

Humility can be a powerful tool for maintaining groundedness. It encourages individuals to acknowledge their limitations, learn from others, and remain open to new experiences, ultimately fostering a sense of connection and appreciating the value of contributions from various sources. Being humble doesn't mean downplaying your achievements or lacking confidence; it means staying grounded, being open to learning, and valuing the contributions of others.

Many people mistakenly believe that humility is a sign of weakness or self-doubt. In reality, it is one of the greatest strengths a person can have. A humble individual acknowledges their accomplishments but also recognises that success is rarely achieved alone. They appreciate the value of teamwork, listen to feedback, and continue to grow.

A person who remains grounded treats everyone with kindness and respect, regardless of their status. This creates a positive work environment, encourages teamwork, and enhances overall productivity. A humble person never assumes they know everything. Instead, they see every experience as an opportunity to grow. The most successful individuals in any industry are those who embrace lifelong learning. They seek feedback, acknowledge mistakes, and adapt to change.

**Some of the world's most influential leaders are known for their humility. For instance:**

- **Warren Buffett**, one of the richest people in the world, still lives in the same modest house he bought in 1958. He credits his success to lifelong learning and staying grounded.
- **Satya Nadella**, the CEO of Microsoft, transformed the company by fostering a culture of empathy, inclusivity, and continuous learning. His leadership style emphasises humility and collaboration.

- **Mahatma Gandhi**, a leader who changed the world, always lived a simple life and remained humble despite his enormous influence.

These examples show that true success doesn't require arrogance or self-promotion—it comes from wisdom, resilience, and a humble approach to leadership.

**Practical Tips to Stay Humble While Achieving Great Things**

1. **Acknowledge Others' Contributions** - Recognise and appreciate the efforts of those around you. Success is a team effort.
2. **Stay Open to Feedback** - Constructive criticism helps you grow. Listen, learn, and improve.
3. **Practice Gratitude** - Remind yourself of the journey and those who helped you along the way. Gratitude keeps you grounded.
4. **Keep Learning** - No matter how much you achieve, there's always more to learn. Stay curious and open-minded.
5. **Avoid Seeking Validation** - True confidence doesn't come from boasting. Let your work speak for itself.

**Conclusion**

Staying humble doesn't mean thinking less of yourself; it means thinking of yourself less and focusing on continuous growth, learning, and collaboration. Success is not just about reaching the top—it's about lifting others along the way and maintaining the respect of those around you. By staying grounded, you ensure that your success is not just temporary but lasting and meaningful.

# 14

# The Right Usage of Wealth

**WEALTH IS AN** indispensable aspect of one's life. In today's world, you cannot buy even the necessities of life if you don't have money. Even a renunciate who claims that he has forsaken the world has to beg to satisfy his daily needs. So many books have been written on the concept of money. Whether it is '*Think and Grow Rich*' by Napoleon Hill or '*Rich Dad, Poor Dad*' by Robert Kiyosaki, they all teach us how to accumulate as much wealth as possible.

In this chapter, I am going to elucidate my perspective related to wealth. I love money. I love a luxurious life. I don't like travelling in overcrowded trains and buses. I don't like eating junk food. I prefer to eat organic food and dried fruits, which are relatively expensive. I want to learn new languages like French and Japanese. The cost of learning French can vary greatly depending on the method and location. Formal courses through institutions like universities or language schools can range from INR 1,000 to INR 60,000 or more. Online resources and apps can offer free or low-cost options, while tutoring may be more expensive. The crux is that to learn something, we require money.

I consider myself a lifelong learner. As I have already discussed in my earlier chapter, I want to learn the flute, become a chess grandmaster and learn foreign languages. But to pursue my passion, I require a good amount of wealth. So, yes, money is required if you want to achieve anything substantial in life.

However, we must never be greedy after wealth and affluence. I was greedy for money once upon a time. I only wanted cash and nothing else. I wanted to live in a larger house which has all the amenities. I wanted to dine in posh restaurants. I wanted fancy cars and luxurious watches. But this greediness took a toll on my mental health. I couldn't achieve my dreams because I encountered a lot of fiascos in my life.

My parents took me to a mental hospital because I was throwing tantrums in my house. In reality, I had everything in my life. My parents owned a 3 BHK flat in Navi Mumbai. My parents also owned a 2 BHK flat in Kerala. My father was working in the Income Tax Department and earned good money. I belonged to an upper-middle-class background. But I was greedy. I was not happy with my life because I wanted to live a luxurious life.

Today, my overall perspective about wealth has changed. Money is important, but more than money, peace of mind is important. You may be surrounded by all sorts of luxuries, but if you don't have peace of mind, then all your creature comforts are worthless. On the other hand, you may be living a minimalistic lifestyle, but if you are having peace of mind, then you are living a worthwhile life.

Matthieu Ricard, known as "the world's happiest man," generally views money as a potential distraction from deeper values and a source of suffering when pursued excessively. He argues that happiness is not found in wealth or material possessions but in inner peace, altruism, and a sense of purpose. He believes that an overemphasis on material wealth can lead to dissatisfaction, anxiety, and a lack of genuine connection with others. Ricard argues that true happiness comes from cultivating inner peace, practising compassion, and engaging in activities that align with one's values, rather than pursuing material gain.

However, I don't believe that money is a source of suffering. Money can also act as a blessing to mankind if it is used for a good purpose. Money can provide access to better living conditions, opportunities, and resources that can improve people's lives, and it can also be a tool for positive change and progress in society.

Money can enable people to access better food, housing, healthcare, education, and other necessities, leading to a higher quality of life. Financial resources can open doors to education, entrepreneurship, and other opportunities that can lead to personal and professional growth. Money can be used to fund charities, invest in research, and support initiatives that address social problems and promote positive change in the world. Money plays a crucial role in driving economic growth, creating jobs, and improving overall living standards for many people.

It all depends on how you use your money. Money can be a source of evil, too. Money can exacerbate inequalities, leading to unfair advantages for some and exploitation of others. An excessive focus on wealth can lead to materialism and a disregard for non-material values like compassion and social justice. Money can corrupt individuals and institutions, leading to unethical behaviour and a lack of accountability.

Atman in Ravi (AiR), also known as a business tycoon turned monk, emphasises that while money is important, it's not the ultimate goal of life. He suggests that the real source of happiness lies in developing inner values like peace, purpose, and fulfilment. AiR believes that true happiness comes from transcending the pursuit of fleeting pleasures and engaging in meaningful actions that contribute to the collective good.

### *AiR's perspective on money can be summarised in a few key points:*

- **Money as a tool, not a goal:**

He sees money as a means to an end, not the end itself. It can be used to provide for one's needs and wants, but it cannot buy true happiness or fulfilment.

- **The importance of "clean money":**

AiR suggests that it's crucial to make money ethically and responsibly. He emphasises the importance of using money to benefit others and contribute to society.

- **Happiness beyond possessions:**

He believes that true happiness comes from finding inner peace, purpose, and meaning, not from accumulating wealth or material possessions.

- **The power of good karma:**

AiR emphasises that the most valuable "currency" is good karma, which transcends material existence. He encourages individuals to use their resources and influence to do good and make a positive impact on the world.

AiR's teachings are based on the idea that true happiness requires shifting our focus from external rewards to internal growth and fulfilment. He suggests that by developing inner values and engaging in meaningful actions, we can find a deeper and more lasting sense of happiness.

Watch this 3-minute YouTube video of Atman in Ravi entitled 'Is money the only source in today's life to achieve satisfaction?':

https://www.youtube.com/watch?v=Lz8zg41DbEI

In conclusion, earn money ethically and build your wealth. But never be greedy for money. Use a small part of your wealth (at least 10 per cent of your monthly earnings) for a good purpose and earn 'Good Karma'. Spend money on upgrading yourselves by learning new skills. Use your money on buying salubrious food that will help you improve your overall health and well-being. Then you see how money can help you to fulfil all your good aspirations.

# 15

# Death is the Ultimate Truth of Life

**EVERYONE WHO IS** born in this material world is going to die one day. Whether you are the richest king or the poorest beggar, you are bound to die one day. I am not talking about the eight 'Chiranjeevis' or the immortals of the Hindu Mythology, which include Ashwatthama, Maharaja Bali, Vyasa, Hanuman, Vibhishana, Kripacharya, Parashurama, and Markandeya. I am talking about an individual soul like you and me who is born into this world carrying all sorts of '*Samskara Vasanas*'.

Sadhguru's '*Death: An Inside Story*' challenges conventional views of death, presenting it not as a tragedy but as a natural process and a potential opportunity for transformation. The book encourages a shift in perspective, urging readers to embrace death rather than fear it and to view life as a journey that culminates in this natural transition. It emphasises that death is not the end but a continuation, offering a chance to release attachments and explore new possibilities.

My overall perspective on death changed after reading Sadhguru's incredible book. The book encourages readers to see death as a potential opportunity for transformation and a return to a state of greater awareness. Life and death are interconnected, and viewing death as a natural progression can help individuals live more fully in the present moment. The book suggests that understanding death can help people detach from attachments to the physical body and the material world. Sadhguru emphasises the importance of the breath as a source of life and a reminder of the impermanence of the physical form.

One thing is certain. You cannot determine death. You cannot determine how long you will live. Michael Jackson wanted to live to be 150 years old and took significant measures to try and achieve that goal. He reportedly employed a team of doctors, rigorously monitored his diet, and pursued various treatments and techniques to extend his life. He had a large medical team, including 12 doctors, who were present at his home to monitor his health daily. His food was meticulously tested in a laboratory before being served. He reportedly researched and explored various methods and treatments for extending lifespan, including potential organ donors. Despite his efforts and the extensive medical facilities, Michael Jackson died at the age of 50 on June 25, 2009, from acute propofol intoxication.

In Hinduism, after death, the soul, or atman, is believed to be reborn in another life, a process known as reincarnation. This cycle of birth, death, and rebirth, called samsara, continues until the soul achieves liberation (moksha) from the cycle. The soul's next incarnation is influenced by its karma from previous lives, meaning the actions and deeds of the individual shape their future rebirth.

In Islam, it is *Allah* who decides when a person dies. Most Muslims believe that when they die, they will stay in their graves until **Yawm al-din** (the Day of Judgement). On that day, they will be raised from their graves and brought before Allah and judged on how they lived their earthly lives. This belief is known as the **resurrection of the body**. Those who have performed more good deeds than bad will enter **Jannah** (Paradise). Jannah is a place described as a **"garden of everlasting bliss"** and a **"home of peace"**. In Jannah, there will be no sickness, pain or sadness. Those who have performed more bad deeds than good will enter **Jahannam** (Hell). This is a place of physical and spiritual suffering.

In Christianity, after death, the soul separates from the body and enters a waiting period in the spirit world until the resurrection. The soul then faces judgment, and those who have lived a good life following Christ's example will enter heaven, experiencing eternal life with God. Those who have sinned may go to hell, a place of separation from God and torment.

In Buddhism, death is viewed as a transition rather than an end. It's seen as part of the continuous cycle of rebirth called samsara. Consciousness, or the spirit, is believed to continue after death, and individuals are reborn into new lives, potentially in different realms or forms. The goal of Buddhism is to break free from this cycle and achieve Nirvana, a state of enlightenment and liberation.

In Jainism, the soul, also known as '*jiva*' or '*Ātman*', is considered eternal and does not die. Upon death, the soul leaves the physical body and is reborn into a new body, which may be human, animal, plant, or even a hellish or heavenly form, depending on the individual's karma. This process of rebirth continues until the soul achieves liberation, called '*moksha*', and is free from the cycle of birth and death.

In Sikhism, death is viewed as a natural process and God's will, part of the soul's journey back to God. The physical body is seen as an 'empty vessel', while the soul continues its journey through reincarnation until it attains union with God. The focus of a Sikh funeral is not on mourning but on celebrating the soul's return to God.

In nearly all religions, death is seen as a transitional process, with one's future rebirth shaped by the law of karma. If you have done adequate good karma in your current life, then you need not fear death. But if you have done a lot of bad karma in your current life, then you will face the consequences, whether you like it or not. If you do '*Prayaschit*' for your wrongdoing, then a certain part of your bad karma can be nullified. '*Prayaschit*' is a Sanskrit and Hindi word that generally translates to atonement, penance, or expiation. It signifies the act of making amends for wrongdoing, confessing sins, and seeking forgiveness through various means, often to reduce karmic consequences.

'Memento mori', a Latin phrase meaning 'remember that you must die', is a concept that encourages the remembrance of death as a reminder of the inevitability of mortality. This practice, which has roots in various cultures and historical periods, can be used to help individuals appreciate the present moment, make more meaningful choices, and prepare for their own passing.

### *Why Remember Death?*

- **Appreciating Life:**

By acknowledging the finite nature of life, one can develop a deeper appreciation for the present and the experiences it offers.

- **Making Meaningful Choices:**

The contemplation of death can help individuals align their actions with their values and goals, ensuring their lives are lived with purpose.

- **Preparing for the End:**

Reflecting on death can encourage individuals to address unfinished business, make peace with their relationships, and prepare for the transition from life to death.

- **Reducing Worldly Anxiety:**

Remembering death can help individuals to understand that worldly possessions and accomplishments are temporary, thus reducing their attachment to material things and helping them find more lasting meaning.

- **Promoting Mindfulness:**

The practice of 'memento mori' can encourage mindfulness and present moment awareness, allowing individuals to fully engage with their lives.

### *How to Practice 'Memento Mori'*

- **Meditation and Contemplation:**

Engaging in regular meditation or reflective journaling about death can help cultivate a deeper understanding of mortality.

- **Visiting Graveyards or Burial Sites:**

Visiting places where people have passed away can serve as a visual reminder of the inevitability of death.

- **Focusing on the Present:**

Making conscious choices to appreciate the present moment and engage fully in life's experiences can help in acknowledging and embracing the finite nature of existence.

- **Reading and Learning:**

Exploring resources on death and dying, such as books, articles, or documentaries, can expand one's knowledge and understanding of the topic.

- **Engaging in Conversations:**

Having open and honest conversations about death with loved ones can help create a space for emotional support and shared reflection.

'Maraṇasati', which translates to 'mindfulness of death', is a Buddhist meditation practice focused on contemplating death and the impermanence of life. It involves remembering that death is inevitable and can occur at any moment, prompting a sense of urgency and diligence in practising the Dharma. This practice is not about fearing death, but rather about understanding its reality and using that understanding to cultivate mindfulness and a deeper appreciation for life.

Death is the ultimate truth of life. If you appreciate life, then you will also appreciate death. If you have done a lot of good karma in your life, then you need not fear death. Only a sinner fears death. A saint dies with a smile on his face. From today onwards, take a resolution to mend your old bad habits. Life is short and unpredictable. Death is inevitable. Hence, stop complaining about life and make full utilisation of your time in doing good karma and spreading peace and harmony.

*"Life is eternal, and love is immortal, and death is only a horizon; and a horizon is nothing save the limit of our sight."*

**– Rossiter Worthington Raymond**